Underwater Adventures with Louis and Louise

by Stephen T. Schram

Illustrations by Kimberly VanDenBerg

Brock,

Take a swim with Louis
and Louise and enjoy
meeting all the fish in
their neighborhood.

Stephen T. Schram

Published by Orange Hat Publishing 2015

ISBN 978-1-937165-85-7

Printed in the United States of America

www.orangehatpublishing.com

*To those who appreciate
the Great Lakes fishery*

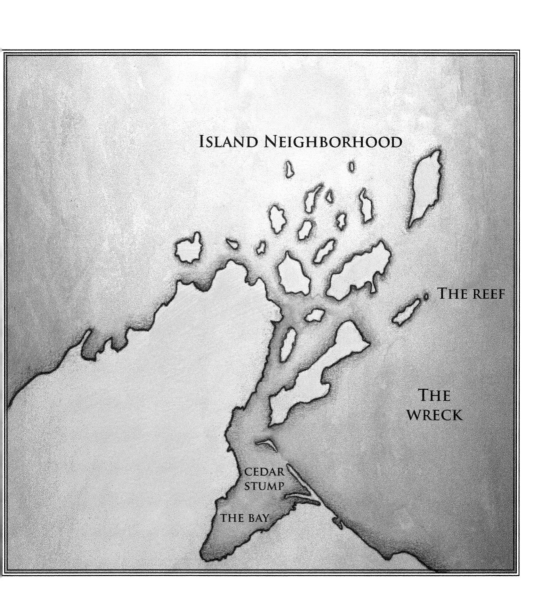

PART 1

Louis and Louise
Meet Their Neighbors

Chapter 1

Laker Lessons

Louis and Louise lived at the bottom of the most magnificent freshwater lake in the world: Lake Superior. The brother and sister duo were lake trout; their friends simply called them lakers. The water in their neighborhood remained cold throughout the year, with a temperature barely above freezing. Sunlight couldn't penetrate the deep depth, so a constant darkness covered their home. This cold, dark neighborhood didn't appeal to all fish, but lakers loved it.

Louis and Louise spent their time eating and being with their friends. One day while playing games, some of the other lakers started making fun of Billy, a large burbot, and Sammy, a small spoonhead sculpin.

"Stop calling them names," pleaded Louis.

But no one listened.

Despite repeated attempts to get the other lakers to stop, the teasing continued, and it became obvious Billy and Sammy had hurt feelings. Louis and Louise felt frustrated and didn't know what to do. They liked playing with all of their friends, but the fun stopped when the teasing started. They decided to leave their neighborhood to find Grandpa Mack and ask him for advice.

Louis and Louise found Grandpa Mack at the reef where he was preparing for the spawning season. They saw the sun's rays shining down from the surface, adding emerald streaks to the shallow water. The reef looked beautiful to them and very different from the dark neighborhood they called home.

"Why are you playing in shallow water today?" asked Grandpa Mack. Mack was short for mackinaw, another name for lake trout.

Louis said, "We were playing games with our friends when some of the other lakers started making fun of Billy and Sammy."

"Tell me what happened," said Grandpa Mack.

Louise quickly responded, "The other lakers called Billy ugly because he has a long whisker below his chin, and they laughed at Sammy because they said spoonhead is a funny name. We asked them to stop, but they wouldn't. Can you tell us what to do?"

Grandpa Mack listened carefully. "We must always consider the consequences before we speak, respecting everyone despite how they might look or if they have a different name. All fish are special in their own way. Each of your friends makes an important contribution to our neighborhood. Remember, just because lakers are top predators doesn't give them the right to bully other fish."

Louise said, "I would rather play with fish who are friendly and happy."

Grandpa Mack continued, "You are wise to spend time with friends who make you feel good. They help you keep a positive attitude, which is an important part of life."

Louise smiled. "Thanks for your good advice."

As they headed for home, the current started

pulling algae off the reef.

"What's happening?" Louis asked Grandpa Mack.

"There's a storm on the surface. Fall storms create strong currents that remove algae from the reef. When we are spawning, our eggs fall into spaces between the boulders. It's important the reef is free of algae so our eggs can develop in clean water. Our eggs must stay between the boulders until they hatch in the spring. Did you notice the brilliant reddish-orange color of my fins?" Grandpa Mack asked proudly. "The spawning season is a very exciting time for lakers, and I enjoy displaying my fall spawning colors."

"Surely your colors will impress the females," smiled Louise, "but what about your scars?"

Grandpa Mack said he'd had the scars for a long time. "Many years ago, a new neighbor, called a sea lamprey, attacked me by attaching himself near my fins," Grandpa Mack continued. "At the time, I was twenty years old. Having a long, wiggly fish hanging on my side bothered me. Eventually the sea lamprey let go and swam away. This unpleasant experience didn't make any sense, so I decided to investigate by getting captured in a net during the spawning season. Normally we view people above the surface as predators, but I took a chance because I wanted some answers. After being pulled to the surface, a scientist examined my scars and inserted a small tag in my back before putting me back in the water. Last fall, during our spawning season, I decided to go back above the surface again because our neighborhood still contained sea lamprey. I wanted to show the scientists my new scars. I thought it might help them realize what was happening to us. After examining my tag, the scientists discovered they tagged me thirty years ago! We looked each other in the eye and had quite a conversation despite not speaking. I received another tag before a scientist took my picture and released me back into the water. I learned that lots of people are working hard to reduce the number of sea lamprey in the lake. It's a big job, so we need to be patient. Fishery scientists help keep our neighborhood healthy. Our survival depends on their work."

"Wow!" said Louise. "Do you think you made a difference?"

Grandpa Mack smiled at her youthful enthusiasm. "I know I made a difference. Changes that happen under water often go unnoticed by people above the surface, because they can't see us. In a way, our world is a mystery to them. If they learned about our problems, they could do a better job taking care of us and our neighborhood. We need to help them understand our underwater world."

After talking to Grandpa Mack, Louis and Louise felt much better.

"Thanks for the visit, Grandpa Mack," said Louis.

Remembering the lessons they learned, the duo returned to deeper waters.

Chapter 2

Sturgeon Stories

Just for fun, Louis and Louise swam to the shallow part of the bay. Usually they stayed in their cold deepwater neighborhood, but today doing something different sounded better.

As the sun set, all the fish in the bay seemed exceptionally excited, so Louis stopped Scotty, a smallmouth bass, and asked why.

"Don't you know?" exclaimed Scotty. "Whenever there is a full moon, everyone heads to the cedar stump in the middle of the bay for an evening of sturgeon stories. A big cedar tree washed out of a river over a hundred years ago and the stump has been sitting on its side in the middle of the bay ever since. It's a perfect location to tell stories when moonbeams reflect off the twisted roots that fan out toward the surface. The sturgeon family started the tradition years ago, and now everyone is welcome. You can tell a funny story, talk about your problems, or just listen."

Johnny Darter swam by and said, "Come on, Scotty, we're heading to the cedar stump. The whole gang from the neighborhood will be there. Don't be late."

Louis and Louise followed Scotty, and within minutes, they took their place around the cedar stump. Fish of all sizes gathered: rock bass, northern pike, walleye, brook stickleback, and minnows. Soon a very large lake sturgeon arrived. Louis and Louise had never seen such a big fish.

"Wow!" said Louis. "Who's that?"

"We don't know his name," replied Scotty." We just call him The Big Guy."

Filled with excitement, Louis and Louise could barely keep their fins still. The Big Guy spoke first, and something magical began. He welcomed Louis and Louise and said he wanted to talk about changes in the neighborhood. Discouraged by the amount of sand being flushed from rivers into the bay, The Big Guy seemed sad. He said sand was burying their neighborhoods and forcing fish to find new homes in other parts of the bay. The sand also buried the rocky shoals in the river where his family went to spawn.

Johnny Darter had been listening under the cedar stump and came out to offer his thoughts on the sand problem. Johnny Darter barely measured two inches long, compared to The Big Guy, who stretched out more than six feet. The Big Guy listened politely. Louis and Louise remembered what Grandpa Mack said about respecting everyone and realized The Big Guy had respect for Johnny Darter despite their enormous difference in size.

Johnny Darter went on to say the sand had buried parts of his neighborhood too. Sticks, logs, and rocks, which were important for his survival, had disappeared over the years. His family had to keep moving to find the right habitat in which to live. He expressed frustration about the sand but couldn't offer a solution.

Then Mary, a mayfly, came out from under the cedar stump. She agreed with Johnny Darter about the increase in sand. Her life changed too, because her family depended on the natural mud in the bottom of the bay. She explained how her family lived in the mud for the first part of their lives. The second part would start very soon. Mary's family planned to rise to the surface and fly away.

What a thrill, thought Louis and Louise, to be able to burrow in the mud for part of your life and fly above the water for the other part.

Scotty spoke next. He talked about his family's favorite game of tug. When they saw a rubber worm or plastic fish attached to a line, they bit it, and someone pulled from the other end. The bass tugged back and the game began. They held on tight and darted around logs and weeds, eventually getting pulled to the surface and into a boat. After humans released them back into the water, the game started again. Scotty said it was fun but sometimes they didn't feel like playing, so they just watched the rubber worms and plastic fish drift by.

All through the night, Louis and Louise sat mesmerized as they listened to stories and watched moonbeams reflect off the cedar stump.

As the moon began to disappear over the horizon, a family of lake sturgeon announced that they were excited to leave the bay. Several generations before, they lived in a river down the shore, but the water became so polluted they had to move. Now the water was clean again, so they were returning to start a new life in the neighborhood where their ancestors used to live. Everyone wished them well and gave them a fin shake before they swam off.

Finally, The Big Guy thanked everyone for another successful night of sturgeon stories. "We didn't solve all of our problems," he explained, "but we shared our feelings and had fun; that's what is important." Louis and Louise enjoyed spending time in the bay, but the warm water forced them to head for home just when the moon set and the sun started coming up.

Chapter 3

New Neighbors

During their travels, Louis and Louise noticed new fish species in their deepwater neighborhood and also in shallow waters of the bay. Some new species weren't even fish; some were zooplankton—tiny animals that drift near the surface—while others were new types of vegetation that swayed with the currents. These new species were the talk of the neighborhood, since they competed for food and seemed to be increasing in abundance. Everyone wanted to know where they came from and how long they planned to stay. Louis and Louise decided to talk to the new neighbors.

Louise began, "Hi, I'm Louise. We noticed you are new to the neighborhood. My brother Louis and I were curious to know where you came from."

A small fish said, "My name is Ralph and I'm a round goby."

Ralph told Louis and Louise his family used to live in a similar neighborhood far away. When his ancestors were very young, some of them were sucked into a ship. They were trapped and couldn't get out. The ship began a long journey across the ocean. Without much to eat and with little oxygen, they barely survived. Eventually they were discharged into a new neighborhood. They wanted to leave but had no idea how to go about getting home. Instead, they decided to make the best of a bad situation by enjoying their new home. Once they adjusted to their surroundings, they thrived. Ralph said most of the fish didn't like them because they ate the same food as native species.

Louise told Ralph about Grandpa Mack going above the surface and making scientists aware of sea lamprey attaching to lakers and scarring their bodies. "Maybe they could solve your problem. Grandpa Mack said we must always remain hopeful that scientists will recognize our situations and help."

Ralph felt a sense of relief. He couldn't wait to tell his family the good news. They might not be able to return to their family home, but scientists might prevent other relatives from being taken from their old neighborhood.

"We want to be your friends," said Louis.

Ralph was thrilled to hear this! Knowing he had two new friends made this a very special day. "Thank you for being so kind!" said Ralph with a joyful voice.

Louis said, "We can never have too many friends."

"Louis and I will come back and visit you as soon as we can," replied Louise.

As Ralph watched Louis and Louise swim away, he didn't feel sad, because he knew these friends would return.

Chapter 4

Safe Swimming

"Let's go to the refuge today," Louis said to Louise.

Louis and Louise loved adventures, but they also enjoyed spending time in the refuge, because it made them feel safe. The refuge stretched out for miles and offered plenty of fish to eat, but mostly it provided protection from getting caught in nets. Grandpa Mack said the refuge was critical to their survival. Fish could rest and grow old in peace.

Louis and Louise met their friend Wyatt, a lake whitefish. Wyatt said his grandfather lived mostly in the refuge, and that's why he was fifty years old, just like Grandpa Mack.

While relaxing in the refuge, a family of spoonhead sculpins swam past and they saw their friend Sammy. "Everyone is heading to the wreck," said Sammy. "The lakers and lake whitefish are going to have a race. The whole neighborhood will be there to watch."

Wyatt suggested they join in the fun, so the three friends headed for the wreck.

About one hundred fifty years ago, a sailing vessel suddenly fell from the surface of the lake and landed right in the middle of the neighborhood. Apparently the vessel sank when a storm filled it with water. The wreck, as everyone called it, had been used for games

ever since. Sammy especially liked hide-and-seek because his small size enabled him to hide where no one could find him. Today, however, wreck racing took center stage, and Sammy volunteered to be the starter.

As the fish lined up, Sammy got into position in a porthole. Besides swimming around the ship, everyone had to swim up and over the ship's bow. The first fish to complete eight laps around the wreck would win the race.

Louis, Louise, and Wyatt took their place at the starting line with other lakers and lake whitefish.

"Go!" yelled Sammy.

The fish started swimming around the outside of the wreck. Up and over the bow they swam, leaving a trail of bubbles behind them.

The lakers and lake whitefish swam so close together it was impossible to tell who was leading. They all crossed the finish line at the same time, so poor Sammy had absolutely no idea who won. He could only see a blur of fish fly past the porthole as the water boiled with bubbles.

Sammy and the other fish decided it didn't matter who won. Everyone enjoyed playing together, and wreck racing was always a great way to exercise and have fun at the same time. Afterward, Louis and Louise laughed with Wyatt and the other fish as they talked about the race. The refuge made everyone feel safe, and laughing together made everyone feel good.

PART 2

Louis and Louise
Discover Underwater Treasure

Chapter 5

Coaster Chet

Louis and Louise always enjoyed swimming along the rocky coast. This neighborhood often had waves crashing on the shoreline, plenty of sunshine, and the chance of meeting new fish. One day, Louis and Louise saw a trout, similar in shape to lake trout, but much more colorful with beautiful black and white markings on the bottom fins.

"Hi, I'm Louis, and this is Louise!" exclaimed Louis proudly. "We are lake trout and live in a deeper and darker neighborhood, quite different from your beautiful home. What's your name?"

"I'm Chester, but my friends and family call me Chet. I'm also a trout, a brook trout. You are called lake trout because you live in the lake. I'm called a brook trout because I live in rivers, which are sometimes called brooks. I spend part of my life in the lake. When I do, I'm called a coaster because I swim near the coast."

"Where's the rest of your family?" Louise was impressed with Chet's knowledge of lakers.

"I'm the only one left," said Chet sadly. "Would you like to hear more of my story?"

Louise quickly responded, "Absolutely."

Chet began by saying his family had a glorious past.

Brightly colored brook trout occupied all the rivers.

After spawning in cool springs, the adults drifted downstream to deep-water resting areas. Many moved to the lake, where forage fish provided plenty of food. A few family members remained in the rivers, but most had disappeared years before, when sand washed off the land and covered their neighborhood. The sand buried spawning grounds, logs, and rocks used by insects that his family relied on for food. Moving downstream, the sand filled deep holes near the river mouths. After a while, brook trout couldn't survive, and most families never returned.

"Would you like to see the problem for yourself?" he asked.

Louis and Louise jumped at the opportunity. "Yes!"

Together the three fish swam to a nearby river. Immediately Louis and Louise sensed danger because their backs were sticking out of the shallow water. Sure enough, sitting on a tree branch high above the water, a bald eagle had been watching them. Suddenly he swooped down, trying to catch his next meal.

"I've seen enough!" cried Louise.

"Me too!" screamed Louis.

In a flash the three friends turned and darted for the safety of the lake just as the eagle's claws came within inches of catching them.

"Whew," sighed Louis. "That was a close call."

"I hope you understand the problem we have with so much sand!" Chet tried to calm his fins after swimming so fast to reach safety. "The river mouth used to have deep pools that provided plenty of hiding places for my family. Now, the water is so shallow I have to be extra careful so predators won't catch me."

Louis and Louise didn't know what to do for Chet, but they tried to offer words of encouragement.

"We can't solve your problem; however, we can be friends and come back to visit," said Louise.

Chet smiled. "I know you can't solve the sand problem. Sometimes I get lonely, so your friendship is very helpful. Thanks for stopping, and please come back soon."

"You can count on us," replied Louis. "Visiting friends is something Louise and I enjoy. We'll be sure to stop the next time we swim along the coastline."

Chapter 6

Pete's Party

"Let's swim to the bay today," Louis suggested to Louise one day.

The bay offered excitement and a chance to see old friends.

After arriving, they saw Pete, a beautiful pumpkinseed. Pete's brilliant colors made him look handsome. Pete told them that it was his birthday and all the fish in the neighborhood would be at his party. He asked Louis and Louise if they would like to come.

"That sounds great," said Louise. "Where do we go?"

Pete replied, "Follow me. I'm on my way right now."

Louis, Louise, and Pete swam to an old dock where all the neighborhood fish waited. The party started as a rock bass named Richard explained the first game: hide-and-seek. Louis and Louise knew this game. They played it in their neighborhood.

Next, Richard taught them a new game called drop the pebble.

Louis held a small pebble in his mouth and had to drop it into a circle on the bottom. The emerald shiner family, led by Elaine, made the circle by moving mud with their fins. The game sounded easy until Richard took a long weed and tied it around Louis's eyes. Now he couldn't see the mud circle at all, so the game quickly became more challenging. Most fish dropped the pebble outside the circle.

For the third game, called flip-and-fly, twin sturgeons, Stu and Sue, formed a straight line as they faced away from each other so that their powerful tails overlapped. Richard hovered over the two tails, and with a quick flip, the gentle giants launched him skyward. Richard disappeared. Before anyone could say anything, the surface exploded. Splash! He fell back into the water. Everyone took turns getting pushed above the surface. Louis and Louise decided to take their turn together.

"Shoot them to the moon!" yelled Pete.

After getting into position, Louis and Louise shot up and out of the water. Looking around, they saw the sun in the sky, trees along the shoreline, and boats tied to a dock. It felt exciting, because everything was new, but the experience scared them because they hadn't been out of the water before. Louis and Louise both did belly flops before swimming back to their friends.

They all took turns, and some fish flew several times.

"Where did you get these ideas for the games?" asked Louise.

"Simple," replied Richard. "I used my imagination."

After playing so hard, everyone had worked up an appetite.

"Let's eat," announced Bob, a slimy bullhead. "I made my specialty: a no-bake critter cake."

Layer upon layer of big, juicy worms rested on

a bed of weeds. The topping consisted of mayflies, dragonflies, and other kinds of bugs found in the area. The cake tasted great and disappeared in no time. Bob laughed as he described how he had collected so many worms by swimming next to the dock where people were fishing and carefully removing the worms from their hooks. He said that he got hooked sometimes and pulled to the surface. The best part was the sound of people screaming when they saw him! They quickly took the hook out of his mouth and let him go. Apparently people above the surface didn't appreciate the beauty of bullheads.

When the party ended, Pete, Elaine, Richard, and Bob thanked Louis and Louise for coming to the birthday celebration. Before swimming home, Louis and Louise told the other fish how they loved playing in the bay and enjoyed spending time with such good friends.

Chapter 7

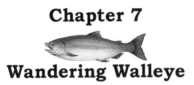

Wandering Walleye

Willy hatched from an egg in a large river along with hundreds of brothers and sisters. His walleye family enjoyed the warm river water and all the good things to eat.

In the middle of the summer, Willy's dad and mother said, "You are old enough to come with us on our summer vacation. It's a long swim, but we think you can handle it."

Willy couldn't wait to get started, and for the next several days his excitement wouldn't let him think of anything else.

"The anticipation of going on a journey is part of the fun," said Willy's mother.

Finally, the journey began. Willy and his parents left the river and started swimming along the shoreline to a wonderful vacation spot with islands, reefs, and lots of fish to eat.

After swimming for several days, Willy started whining, "Dad, I'm getting tired and I'm hungry."

Dad assured him, "We'll stop at a river ahead that has lots of small minnows. We'll stay there for a while to rest and eat."

Ten minutes later, Willy whined again, "Are we almost there yet? It seems we're just wandering

around the lake."

Dad started to tell Willy about the rivers along their route and the importance of knowing which rivers had food and which ones didn't. "It's important to know when and where to stop. It's also important to enjoy our journey."

"He's too hungry to remember anything right now," said Willy's mother.

"Sorry," his dad chuckled, "I forgot that I acted the same way on my first vacation." Eventually they came to the islands, where the waters offered plenty of food. While exploring the new area, Willy met Louis and Louise.

Because Louis and Louise lived in the islands

year round, they couldn't wait to hear about Willy's travels.

"How far did you swim to get here?" Louis asked Willy.

"We started near our home about one hundred kilometers down the shoreline."

Louise wondered, "How far is one hundred kilometers?"

Willy explained that one hundred kilometers was about the same as sixty-two miles.

Louise wanted to know why Willy and his family came to the islands.

"There's a big river," began Willy, "where my family spawns every spring. During the summer, the adults swim to the islands to feed and relax. In the fall, they swim home to prepare for the spring spawning season. This is my first time visiting the islands. My dad told me to enjoy the journey even though I whined about being tired and hungry during the entire swim. Now that we're here and I've had a chance to eat and rest, I feel great."

Willy also said how much he liked having new friends from different parts of the lake. Louis and Louise told Willy about their life in the islands and the other fish they played with every day. They enjoyed playing with Willy and once again remembered Grandpa Mack's advice about spending time with friends who made you feel good.

When fall storms started to blow above the surface, Willy's parents said they needed to head home. Louis and Louise said goodbye to their new friend as Willy swam away. Willy said he couldn't wait to come back next year. Louis and Louise said they would be waiting.

Chapter 8

Deep Dinner

Curiosity led Louis and Louise to a new neighborhood deeper than their home. They could feel the pressure increase on their bodies as they descended to the dark unknown. Arriving at a new neighborhood over six hundred feet below the surface, they discovered trout who looked almost exactly like them.

"Welcome to my home. I'm Frank, a siscowet lake trout," announced a husky fish.

"I'm Louis, and this is Louise. We're exploring and wanted to visit our deepwater neighbors."

Frank said they were closely related, like cousins. Siscowets live in water even deeper than lakers and could survive in this extremely cold neighborhood because they had an extra layer of fat.

"My friends and family call me Frank the Fat. It's not meant in a mean way; it's just a nickname and refers to the fatty layer under my skin."

Frank the Fat told Louis and Louise stories about surviving in his deep, dark home. Life in general was much slower living in such a cold neighborhood. Frank said siscowets didn't grow as fast as regular lakers. They tried to conserve energy, and some years they decided not to spawn.

Just then Louis and Louise noticed several large fish swimming around with fish tails sticking out of their mouths. At first they thought they were strange, mysterious creatures from the deep, but they soon realized they were other siscowets.

"What are they doing?" asked Louise.

"Surviving," responded Frank quickly. "The siscowet family has grown to the point where we don't have a lot of forage fish in our neighborhood anymore, so we have to eat whatever we can, even if it means capturing prey larger than we can swallow. Top predators like us can usually eat a fish up to half our size. However, we have to have confidence to eat a large fish we know we can't completely swallow. We call it having a 'deep dinner.' Eating one very large fish means we have breakfast, lunch, and dinner for at least a couple of weeks. That way we don't have to use extra energy trying to find food."

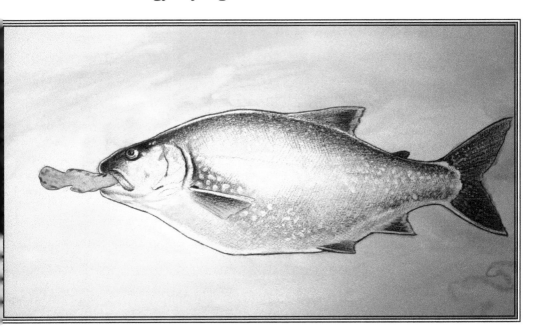

"That's amazing," said Louis. "We have a variety of things to eat in our neighborhood, so we don't have to think about eating a huge fish."

Suddenly, out of the darkness a large siscowet appeared with its mouth wide open. It tried to eat Louise! "Yikes!" she shouted.

"Stop that!" snapped Frank. "Louis and Louise are friends visiting from the islands. Please show our guests some respect."

"Thank you," said a trembling Louise as she worked to compose herself. "That's the first time another fish has tried to eat me."

"Siscowets eat all types of fish, even lakers. We've learned to adapt to our limited food supply by eating other things not found near the bottom of the lake. We are going for a surface swim today to hunt for food. Would you like to join us?"

Louis said, "We would love to come along." As they slowly ascended to the surface, Frank the Fat explained the purpose of a surface swim.

"Sometimes during the summer months, surface winds blow insects and birds over the lake. If they can't fly back to land, they drop to the water. Our job is to find them and start eating. Bumblebees are my absolute favorite," beamed Frank, "but I also eat butterflies, moths, horseflies, and just about anything I can find."

When they couldn't find any more insects, Frank started swimming back to his neighborhood, and Louis and Louise headed home.

"Thanks for the good time," said Louis and Louise.

Frank the Fat used his fins to wave goodbye. "Be sure to come back and visit." As he turned to the other siscowets, he announced, "Having friends like Louis and Louise is a real treasure."

PART 3

Louis and Louise
Explore the Upper Lakes

Chapter 9

Cisco Companions

Louis and Louise felt restless. Being top predators in the greatest lake in the world had its advantages, but they longed for something more.

"I need a new adventure," said Louis.

I'm ready," replied Louise. "Which way?"

"I think we should head east," responded Louis.

So the journey began on a quiet summer morning. Soon the brother and sister duo met a family of deepwater ciscoes who were swimming in the middle of the lake.

"Hi," said Louis. "I'm Louis, and this is my sister Louise. We are lake trout exploring new areas of Lake Superior."

"My name is Bubbles," announced a small cisco. "My family and I are deepwater ciscoes. We are also called chubs and sometimes bloaters. I like to blow bubbles, so my friends call me Bubbles the Bloater Chub. Where did you come from?"

Louise said, "We live in the islands."

Bubbles said his family's neighborhood included an area near the islands along with a large section of the open lake. He invited Louis and Louise to join them as they searched for zooplankton to eat.

Louis and Louise spent the next day swimming

with Bubbles and his family. When they reached the edge of Bubbles's neighborhood, the deepwater ciscoes told Louis and Louise they had to turn around and swim back .

Bubbles the Bloater Chub had a suggestion for Louis and Louise. "If you want to keep heading east, I suggest you swim with my cousins, the shallow water ciscoes or lake herring. Swim up to a shallower depth to meet them."

"Thanks, Bubbles," said Louis. "I think we'll take your advice and continue exploring."

Louis and Louise said goodbye to Bubbles the Bloater Chub and swam upward into warmer water until they met another family of ciscoes. They explained who they were, why they ended up in the middle of the lake, and the advice they received from Bubbles.

"Bubbles is so much fun to be around," announced Charlie, the leader of the cisco family.

Unlike his cousin Bubbles, Charlie's neighborhood extended over a much larger area. He told Louis and Louise they were swimming to the far eastern end of the lake and they were welcome to join them.

"First we are going to eat," Charlie told them. "Every evening, zooplankton rise toward the surface from their deepwater home. We feed on them until morning when they descend again to deep water. It's a real feast."

The ciscoes had small mouths, which made it easy for them to eat tiny zooplankton. Louis and Louise had much larger mouths, for eating fish, so they watched as the ciscoes ate.

After a day of swimming, Charlie showed Louis and Louise the uneven bottom with steep underwater hills and deep valleys plunging to blackness.

"You are over the deepest area in the lake," said Charlie. "It's too deep for our family, but other fish, like burbot, siscowets, and sculpins, live there. Besides fish, life at the very bottom of Lake Superior consists of only a few species of bottom-dwelling invertebrates. Since sunlight can't penetrate that deep, production at the bottom of the food web is restricted, so most animals find it difficult to survive."

Louis and Louise listened eagerly, letting their minds absorb this new information. They loved learning.

The ciscoes continued swimming east until they reached a large bay at the eastern end of Lake Superior. Charlie told them about the possibility of going downstream through a river to another Great Lake. But in order to see the new lake and return to their Lake Superior home, warned the ciscoes, Louis and Louise must travel through the magic box.

"What's the magic box?" asked Louis.

"There is a long, narrow box that allows you to be lowered to the river level below the level of Lake Superior. When you return, you are lifted up to the level of Lake Superior again. It's magic!"

Intrigued, Louis and Louise didn't hesitate making a decision. They decided to seize the opportunity by traveling through the magic box and continuing their journey downstream to the other Great Lake. They said goodbye to the friendly ciscoes and headed downstream into the unknown.

Soon they encountered the magic box. Following the instructions from the cisco family, they waited for the doors to open. Louis and Louise swam inside and headed to the far end, just like the ciscoes told them. The doors closed. Except for light from above, everything went black. Louis and Louise waited as water slowly poured out of the magic box. Soon a different set of doors opened, and Louis and Louise entered a swift current. While swimming downstream, they encountered a small fish hiding behind a large rock.

"Come over behind my rock and rest," said Josie, a small logperch.

"Thanks," said Louise. "We are on our way to explore another lake."

"After you rest, you can continue your journey," said Josie.

Josie told Louis and Louise about the river she called home. "I hide and rest behind my rock. I'm not even two inches long, so this rock provides a perfect place for me. When I'm hungry, I swim into the river and look for food drifting downstream. I've spent my entire life in this small area of the river."

It made sense to Louis and Louise that Josie would live in a small neighborhood. The large rock protected her from the strong current, and her small size meant she didn't need large amounts of food to survive.

Louis said, "Thanks for letting us share your rock. It's time for us to continue our journey."

Louis and Louise said goodbye to Josie and continued swimming downstream until the river entered a large lake. They looked forward to leaving the strong current behind them and swimming in a lake again.

Chapter 10

Stanley's Shadow

Once they escaped the swift current, Louis and Louise swam to deeper water.

"Which way now?" asked Louis.

"Let's head west," Louise replied.

Soon they saw a family of lake whitefish eating along the bottom.

"Hi," beamed Louise. "My brother Louis and I are lakers from Lake Superior, and we are exploring a new lake."

"Welcome to Lake Huron," said a lake whitefish. "My name is Wilma. Come join us for lunch."

While they ate, Louis and Louise noticed Wilma's mouth on the lower part of her head. They remembered their lake whitefish friends eating the same way. Wilma told Louis and Louise about Lake Huron and the fish who live there. Louis and Louise asked Wilma why she was so thin compared to their lake whitefish friends back home.

"After new species of mussels invaded our neighborhood, they filtered large amounts of water containing plankton. It worked well for them because that's how they eat, but it changed the entire food web for us. We used to feed on small, fatty animals that live on the bottom. These animals were impacted by the mussels and started declining, so we started eating mussels, which aren't as nutritious. Without good food, our bodies became thinner."

"Our neighborhood also changed," said Louis. "We have a few mussels but not as many as here."

"I wish we could help," said Louise.

Wilma thanked her for the offer but said there wasn't much anyone could do.

Wilma told Louis and Louise about another lake they should see. But first they had to find a huge lake sturgeon named Stanley because they must pass under 'Stanley's Shadow' in order to reach the next lake.

After a short swim, Wilma introduced Stanley to her new friends.

Stanley looked larger than any lake sturgeon Louis and Louise had ever seen! After introductions, Louis and Louise told Stanley about their journey from Lake Superior and their desire to see another lake.

Louise asked, "Can you help us?"

Stanley smiled. "I'd be happy to help you. Lakes Superior, Huron, and Michigan are called the Upper Lakes. There are other lakes downstream from Lake Huron, but I have only heard stories about them. I live and swim between Lake Huron and Lake Michigan. The narrow passage has strong currents that move food items into shallow water where I like to eat. The passage goes under a shadow that takes you into Lake Michigan. Almost seventy years ago, I remember making the passage without a shadow. One day, a thin, dark line started appearing on the water near each shore. The two shady lines gradually got closer together and finally connected. The shadow appears during the day and when there is a bright moon.

We don't know why it's there, but it's harmless and doesn't bother our movement patterns. Since I'm the only fish alive who remembers the passage before the shadow, everyone in the neighborhood refers to it as Stanley's Shadow."

"That's very interesting," said Louis. "Can Louise and I swim through the passage now?"

"Yes, let's get started," responded Stanley. "Follow me."

Louis and Louise followed Stanley under the shadow into Lake Michigan. Stanley told them to look up when they approached the middle of the passage.

Louis and Louise swam to the surface. Looking up, they could see a long, narrow shape stretching from shore to shore.

"Wow!" said Louise.

"I wonder what it could be?" asked Louis.

"I don't know," said Louise. "Let's keep moving."

"I'm heading over to the shallow flats to look for food," announced Stanley. "If you keep heading west, you'll find reefs, lots of fish, and islands."

That sounded good to Louis and Louise, so they said thank you and goodbye to Stanley.

Chapter 11

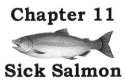

Sick Salmon

Louis and Louise couldn't wait to meet new friends in Lake Michigan. They introduced themselves and shared their journey.

"Nice to meet you," said a small minnow. "My name is Sparkle, and I'm a spottail shiner."

"And I am Albert, an alewife," announced a slightly larger fish.

Sparkle swam fast, and as he did, Louis and Louise could see his body glimmering in the shallow water.

"We noticed the fish in your neighborhood are very excited. What's going on?" inquired Louise.

Albert explained, "The salmon are sick."

"What's wrong?" asked Louis.

"First I have to go back in time to tell our story," began Sparkle. "Years ago, our neighborhood had a natural balance. Then a new neighbor, called sea lamprey, arrived. This fish killed top predators, such as lakers and burbot. It was a dark, sad time in our history. The balance between predator and prey has never been the same."

"That's what happened in our neighborhood," Louise told them. "Fortunately, some of the lakers survived and now our population is healthy again."

"I wish I could say the same about our lake," continued Sparkle.

"When Albert and his family arrived as new neighbors, they thrived without predators. Suddenly an unexpected fish called salmon showed up in large numbers. Now salmon became the top predator and ate members of Albert's family. Things were fine until the alewife started declining."

"Why are alewife declining?" Louise asked Albert.

"Because too many salmon are eating them. Salmon have to eat constantly to grow quickly because their life cycle only lasts a few years."

"Our life cycle is very different than salmon," said Louise. "We don't have to eat all the time because we grow slowly and live for a long time. In fact, our Grandpa Mack is fifty years old. Plus our relative Frank the Fat said some members of his family can eat one big fish and not eat again for a few weeks."

"That's certainly not the case with salmon," said Sparkle. "In order to reach a large spawning size in a few years, they must eat large amounts of nutritious food on a regular basis. If they have to swim long distances and use too much energy without finding food, they get sick."

"It sounds complicated," said Louise.

"Yes, it is. Salmon are still relatively new to this lake, and a new species needs time to adapt. Other new species have also arrived, which changed the entire food web, from the smallest creatures living on the bottom, up to top predators like salmon. The neighborhood still hasn't found a natural balance. Maybe it never will," Sparkle said sadly.

Louis and Louise told Sparkle and Albert about Grandpa Mack visiting with scientists above the surface.

"We also have a problem with sea lampreys," stated Louis. "Perhaps these same scientists can solve your problems too."

"That's good news," said Sparkle.

Sparkle said goodbye to his new friends and hoped they were right about scientists helping to restore the natural balance in the lake.

Chapter 12

Superior Spirit

Louis and Louise decided to swim over to deep water near a reef that looked like a good laker neighborhood. Right away they found a family of lake trout.

"Hi, I'm Liz," announced a laker about the same size as Louis and Louise. "Where did you come from?"

"We are from Lake Superior," responded Louis proudly.

Liz welcomed them to her neighborhood and wanted to hear about their adventures. After telling her, the three lakers decided to talk about differences in their bodies.

"I noticed you don't have one of your fins," said Louise.

"Yes, in fact my entire family has the same fin missing. I also don't know where I was born; I do know I wasn't born in this lake. My family and I were released from someplace above the surface and that's how we came to live here."

"We were born on a reef," said Louise. "My family goes to the same reef to spawn every year."

Liz said her family started going to a reef to spawn, but only a few eggs survived. She didn't know why.

"We'll talk to Grandpa Mack when we return home," said Louis. "He might have the answer."

"Thanks," said Liz.

Liz suggested Louis and Louise visit some of the islands in Lake Michigan.

"Great idea," said Louis.

After saying their goodbyes to Liz, Louis and Louise headed to the nearby islands. Instead of finding lakers, they found shallow water and fish species similar from the bay back home.

"I'm Spanky," announced a smallmouth bass. "Welcome to my island playground."

"When we heard about these islands, we thought the water would be deeper with lake trout in the neighborhood," said Louis.

"These islands are surrounded by shallow water and are home to smallmouth bass," said Spanky. He said the bass liked to play games with hooks that had minnows or plastic worms attached.

"That's exactly the same game our friend Scotty plays back home," said Louise.

"We bite the minnow and someone pulls us around as we dart up, down, and around logs," said Spanky. "We love to pull hard, but when we have had enough, we spit the hook out and swim back to deeper water. We have lots of fun! At the end of the day, my family and I talk about how many times we spit out hooks. I always say we spanked whoever is on the other end of the line. That's why my family calls me Spanky."

Louise noticed a tag near Spanky's dorsal fin. "Where did you get that tag?"

"Many members of my family have tags. Besides playing with hooks, we also get caught in nets, pulled above the surface, and inspected by scientists before being released back into the water. We each receive a tag."

"That's exactly what happened to our Grandpa Mack!" said Louis.

Spanky replied, "We're not sure what it all means, but it doesn't bother us."

"Grandpa Mack told us that the information from tagging helps scientists study our lives," remarked Louise. "For example, if you are captured again at a different location, they know where you were tagged and how far you moved. I'm sure tagging will help your family as well."

After spending the day with Spanky, the warmer water around the islands started to make Louis and Louise long to head back to cooler depths. "Maybe we should think about going home," suggested Louis.

"This has been quite a journey," added Louise. "I'm ready to go home too."

They said goodbye to Spanky, and as they prepared to leave Lake Michigan, they saw Sparkle again.

Sparkle wished them safe travels. "I'm glad I met both of you. Even though you are large fish and top predators, you have respect for everyone, even a small minnow like me. You know how to enjoy life, you are friendly and kind, and you have a positive attitude. You have 'Superior' spirit."

"Thanks for the kind words," answered Louise. "Louis and I have enjoyed our adventure exploring new waters and especially meeting so many new friends. We will always remember you."

Louis and Louise said goodbye to Sparkle and started the long journey back to their island home. First they swam under Stanley's Shadow to get back into Lake Huron. Then they swam up a river past Josie's rock before entering the magic box. This time, water filled the magic box and lifted them up to the level of Lake Superior. They swam part of the way with a group of ciscoes before heading back to their island home.

When they reached the islands after several days of traveling, the first thing they did was find Grandpa Mack. He listened as Louis and Louise talked about the friends they made on their journey to the Upper Lakes. They found some fish living in large neighborhoods and others spending their entire lives in neighborhoods so small it seemed hard to imagine. Louis and Louise told him fish in the other lakes lived similar lives. They faced different problems with new species. Some fish couldn't find enough to eat and became sick. Healthy food was abundant in the islands, but it was sometimes a problem in the other lakes. Those neighborhoods needed help from scientists above the surface.

As Louis and Louise continued talking into the night, Grandpa Mack smiled to himself. He knew Louis and Louise remembered the laker lessons he taught them and he realized their experience made them appreciate their home. More importantly, Louis and Louise would continue to take care of their neighborhood. And that made Grandpa Mack beam with pride!

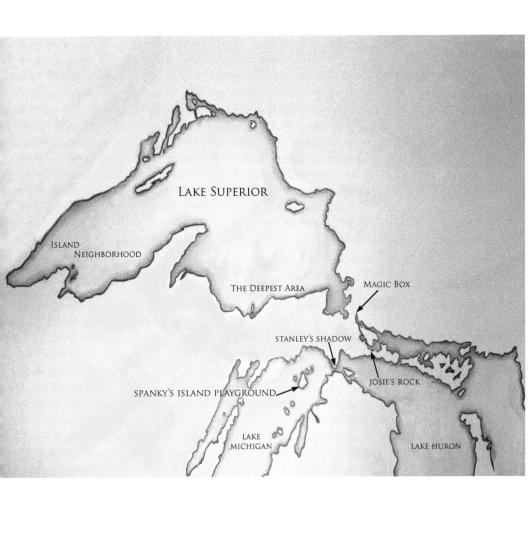

Glossary

Algae – Microscopic plants usually drifting with the current.

Food Web – Interconnecting food chains.

Forage Fish – Small fish eaten by bigger fish.

Habitat – The place where plants or animals live.

Invertebrates – Small animals without a backbone.

Lake Huron – One of the five Great Lakes bordered by the State of Michigan and the Province of Ontario, Canada.

Lake Michigan – One of the five Great Lakes located entirely within the United States.

Lake Superior - The largest of the Great Lakes bordered by the United States and the Province of Ontario, Canada.

Magic Box – The locks at Sault Ste. Marie, Michigan, used to raise or lower ships and fish between Lakes Huron and Superior.

Native Species – Species that live in the habitat where they evolved.

Plankton – Microscopic plants or animals drifting with the current.

Predators – Bigger fish that eat smaller fish.

Prey – Smaller fish that are eaten by bigger fish.

Scientist – A person who studies science, such as fisheries biology.

Spawning season – The time of year when fish lay their eggs.

Stanley's Shadow – The shadow from the Mackinac Bridge, which connects Upper Michigan and Lower Michigan.

Zooplankton – Microscopic animals eaten by forage fish.